AWAKE THE MIGHTY MEN

WHY THE SANCTITY OF LIFE IS ALSO A MAN'S FIGHT, AND SEVEN ACTIONS HE CAN TAKE TO WIN IT.

MIKE G. WILLIAMS

Other Books by Mike G. Williams

Turkey Soup For The Sarcastic Soul, Vol. 1

Turkey Soup For the Sarcastic Soul, Vol. 2

Life Happens: Shut Up, Smile, and Carry a Plunger

An Amateur's Guide to Skunk Repair

Men Moved To Mars When Women Started

Killing The Ones on Venus

Love Is Not A Three Letter Word

Don't Stand Under A Flock Of Angry Birds

100% of the profit from this book will go directly to
fund pregnancy resource centers throughout the world.

ISBN: 1505538521
ISBN-13: 978-1505538526

CONTENTS

CHAPTER 1

MEN, MEN, MEN, MEN...

*"Right or wrong, this planet will most likely always
be controlled by those with upper body strength."*
-James Dobson

I am a man. A MAN! Beyond the parts that require fig leaves in a Bible story picture book, I am also an emotionally strong and physically tough dude. I hunt, I fish, I ride motorcycles, I watch football, I like to lay around in my underwear on occasion and find no fault in it. I rather enjoy it.

I am not "offended" (whatever that means anymore) by your choice of adjectives or adverbs. I know how to jump start a car and siphon gas through a garden hose. I built a successful business on hard work, and long hours, and blood, and sweat, and no crying.

I come from a long heritage of strong men who fought in World Wars, and won them. I really enjoy what John Eldredge wrote in describing the soul of a man. He based an entire book around the belief that men are and should be... Wild At Heart.

This book is not a religious book. I hold firmly to some very strong fundamental personal religious beliefs, but that is beside the point of most of the arguments. You should not be offended by my lack of religious content, nor afraid of its inclusion. I will include a few clearly Biblically based observations in this book, because I can.

I am writing this book in my own words. There will be no editor to change the wording to be more kind and inclusive. There will be no spell or grammar checker other than what is offered by the computer. Are you okay with that? I'm writing as one grammatically-challenged man to another.

I am going to talk to you as real men. I am going to dare you to face a critical issue, to face a giant. I will not criticize or belittle you during our journey. You were created in God's own image. You have my respect.

Men have been lied to. We have been bait-n-switched. We have been deceived. How does that make you feel? I'll bet there still is enough manhood left in our postmodern genes that will allow something inside us to raise our fists and rise for a challenge. You may have been told that the issue at hand is not a man's issue. I intend to prove that was another deception.

This book is about saving lives. It is about the sanctity of life, every life, from womb to tomb! A scary topic for some. This book will discuss the ever heated and debated issue of abortion and a lot more. Please know that I hold no ill feelings to those who have been involved in an abortion in any way. We will all stand before God one day, not before each other. I also believe that God forgives the mistakes of our past. Please absorb no guilt from me in these pages. Never revel in the failures of the past when you can move on to redeem a successful future.

This is my personal challenge... dare... charge... however you wish to receive it... to wake up! You are a mighty man. Face the following facts, observations, or assumptions (you be the judge) and do what a man should do.

I do also welcome any women who dare to look at the hard facts about our common issue. Just be aware that you are in our man cave now. There are no holds barred here (a wrestling phrase). This book does not negate the wonderful work women have done in the fight. Women (by vast majority) have held the battle lines long enough. This book is an invitation for men to add their strengths to the line. Together we are greater than we are individually. I'm sure you agree.

CHAPTER 2

THE INCOMING FIRE

"Wake up the mighty man... prepare for war...
beat your farming tools into battle swords."

-Joel

Soldier, there are children under attack in that building, will you go and defend them? Fireman, there is a little baby in that burning house, will you climb that ladder to rescue that child? Crossing guard, those children have ventured out into the street, will you risk your life to bring them to safety? Dad, a neighboring child has fallen into the pool, will you jump in to save it? Of course all of these men would. So would you. You might think that you do not have the ability, but I'll bet a few bucks that faced with the life-critical dilemma that you would try your hardest. Maybe you would even die trying. In fact for a little child, most would die trying. In fact, children are so important they are the ones we would save first. It is always women and children who are saved first. At least that is how we were taught in our kindergarten manners class.

The problem is that children are dying today. Over 3,000 of them... today. The story will repeat itself tomorrow. They are not dying in a foreign land, but rather in our own land of the free and home of the brave. They are not dying from deceases. They are not dying from auto accidents. Not from SIDS, Cancer, or from a falling tower in New York City. They are dying at the hands of those who find them... inconvenient. The American mother's womb is now the most dangerous place for a human to be. Statistically that is very true. They are dying at the hands of those who profit greatly (a multi-million dollar industry) from their death.

I know that many men secretly, or at least silently, do not know where they stand on abortion. I know that is partly because many of us have had at least a small part in one either knowingly or unknowingly in their high school or college years. You may have chosen to put that out of your mind. We called it what we were told, "The elimination of some tissue." However, down deep in our hearts we knew that we really don't want to stand before a great Creator on that one.

I know that this issue is far spread and touches many. By the time they reach age forty, about 1/3 of all women have had at least one abortion. They didn't get in that situation initially without a man contributing at least two minutes of his time. One can even note that these same stats carry into the church, the choir, and the clergy as well. The Born Again, religious, Protestant, or Catholic experience has not had the impact in this area that we had hoped it would have. Sorry to be so blunt. Your local Pregnancy Resource Center or local Planned Parenthood stats will prove that. The surveys show that a [high] number of women have an abortion who declare to be either a Catholic or a Protestant. Protestant includes all those Baptist, Methodist, Pentecostal, Charismatic, Non-Denominational, and the like. Please keep that in your mind as it will help us to avoid becoming judgmental.

Now I need to stop! I need to stop referring to "these" women who are having abortions as "these" women. They are more than that. They are our nieces, our daughters, and our granddaughters. So from this point on I will try and use those more personalized terms when I speak of the female gender. You need to personalize these issues as well. We can all look more honestly at all things when it comes home to our house. If we can't come up with something that will work at our own house, then we need to be careful placing our yoke on others.

Let's look at the medical facts about abortion. This blob of tissue, as some would call it, has a little more going on than some might think. At three weeks after conception, this extremely human looking blob already contains a full set of DNA from the mother and you. At five weeks the heart is beating at a different rate of speed than that of the babies mom. At eight weeks the arms and legs are growing and the child already has a nose. At ten weeks this future Fisherman has vital organs – such as kidneys, intestines, brain, and liver. Tiny fingernails and toenails are forming. At eleven weeks this future Scientist is almost fully formed as bones are beginning to harden, and genitalia is developing externally. At fourteen weeks this future Carpenter may have discovered thumb-sucking. At fifteen weeks this future Senator can see light that filters in from outside the mother's womb. At nineteen weeks this future football quarterback can hear sounds that come from outside the womb, such as his father's voice. Yet still, the mother in many states can have this future President injected with salt, torn limb from limb, and sucked from the womb for many weeks to come. The womb is now a dangerous game of Russian Roulette.

Thanks to advancement in medical practices, children born prematurely are now more likely to live than to die. Some argue that without the help of doctors these aborted children could never live outside the womb. Correct! Would you consider that without the help of your mother, you as a healthy full term baby would not have survived more than about 72 hours either? So maybe that is a mute point. All of us, whether we are full term or partial term delivery, healthy or sickly, are alive because someone intervened in our life, and at minimum, fed our hungry faces.

Though I am fully capable of understanding that it does take [up to] 48 hours for a boatload of my sperm to find and permeate one little egg, after that we have no question as to the existence of life. Now the sustainability of life is another question. But again, I say we are all, at every age, dealing with a sustainability of life question. I personally can't go more than a few days without my Scientist made – Doctor prescribed - Pharmacy provided - Insurance paid for... heart medications. My point is, the smallest of our male little brothers (and little sisters) are being ripped from the very cavern they were given for safety. This is being done with the permission of those who caused their life to begin in the first place. Since the legalization of abortion in 1973, we have lost over forty million children and the chart is climbing. That is about 130 children exterminated every hour.

Can you tell I believe in the sanctity of life? Especially mine! At no time do I want to be told that my model of person needs to be replaced or discontinued. *I have joked for years that there might be certain people groups that we might be better without. We can all humorously think of a few.* I believe in the sanctity of all human life. In an act of insane boldness I walked onto a pro-life stage a few weeks ago and announced, "I am kinda Pro-Choice*." My audience gasped. I continued, "I simply believe that you need to limit the giving of the "choice" to the child... and that is going to take a few years before we can give it that choice!"

This book is not trying to make a case for whether or not an abortion terminates a life. I meet few educated pro-choice people who would not admit that. Beyond that, anyone who has seen a partial-birth abortion cannot deny that a living baby comes partly out and is terminated at knifepoint. This book is a challenge to you and I as to what we are going to do about the death trap that is the modern womb and what can we do that will [actually] make a difference.

CHAPTER 3

SLEEPING THROUGH WORLD HISTORY CLASS

"Those who cannot remember the past
are condemned to repeat it."
-George Santayana

Who can forget the infamous genocides of the past? Historical record certainly has taught us that mankind, even very religious man can be a cruel murdering tyrant. Who can watch the movie Schindler's List without having a bit of anger well up in them for the inhumane treatment of the Jewish people? Say the word "Auschwitz" and you have immediately put a dark vibe in on the conversation.

As we look at Hitler's ethnic cleansing (killing of Jews) from our postmodern perspective we see the horrendous atrocity. Yet when Hitler propagated it, it seemed to be the right thing to do. There were christian churches (I chose to use a small c in this case) who were supporting this genocide. Some believed they were avenging the death of Jesus, as if God or Jesus needs us to avenge for him. *Apparently they were not avid readers of the book of the Revelation.*

Today we could all go down to a holocaust museum and view the relics of those few who lived through Auschwitz, and those who didn't. We could view the remains, walk the death showers, we could almost smell the smell of death. Some have described the place as demonic. We could look at the names, we could see the photos of the families wiped out. Most of the visitors cry at some point. For many it is gazing upon the children's displays. Why? I will not hide it, you see where I am going. One can compare the 3.3 million Jews lost to the ever increasing 40+ million children aborted, terminated, slaughtered in the United States alone since 1973. Could we call the abortionist office the modern day Nazi Death Camp? The statistics make the tragically inhumane Civil War look rather civil.

I wonder if history will one day include a museum remembering the aborted children of the United States? I wonder if people will walk the halls and read the millions upon millions of names and cry. I wonder if people will ask the same questions they do at the holocaust museums? Will they ask why? Why did a christian nation (note the lowercase c again) turn a blind eye to the senseless slaughter of the innocent? Will they ask why the church has not risen up? Some say this scenario will happen when our country is eventually faced with demise and then rebuilt by those with their hindsight being closer to 20/20. Certainly men can sit here reading and know that we had little to do with all this. This started back in 1973. We men are innocent, and [we] aren't having the abortions.

CHAPTER 4

ON OUR WATCH

*"A man must be big enough to admit
his mistakes, smart enough to profit from them,
and strong enough to correct them."*
-John C. Maxwell

I believe that silent indifference to a murder is complicity to a murder. There comes a point at which those who have not done anything to stop a tragic murderous act should posses a portion of the guilt. Membership in a society itself indicates a pre-ordained mandate to protect all that are within that society.

If I know that someone was going to kill your son or daughter and I did not tell you, I doubt that you would stand in my defense, and fight for my right to keep silent. I'm just saying that when it becomes personal, we all become pragmatists. Let's be honest, you would pull my fingernails out if needed to protect [your] child.

Another reason we hold some responsibility for the current abortion allowances is, though we can't change yesterday (1973), we can change today and tomorrow. Abortion is a nasty repercussion to the loose restraints we have placed on human sexuality in our society. The so called "Free Love Generation" (more properly named the No-Sexual Boundaries Generation) may not have started in my era of control, but it has certainly not been impeded by my generation's involvement. Hey, as a modern man I am more sexually supercharged than every generation before me. I am being sexually stimulated at every turn. It is amazing that I am not raping and pillaging right now instead of writing a book. Your sons and daughters are being more stimulated and supercharged than me.

On our watch the Victoria Secret has paraded the half naked angel commercials almost non-stop across my screen. Commercials that in my adolescent days would have caused me to explode on the spot. The commercial breaks between religious programming are for Viagra and KY Jelly. Our sons and daughters can search Google images without any restriction as if it were a library index file. We are allowing our children to be "hyped up" to "hook-up" with little concern for the outcome. Even many religious parents have resorted to a simple hope that their children will try to use condoms. How is that working?

This blatant supercharging of our sexual society is happening on [our] watch as we recline in our stress-free chair without the slightest effort to change it. Pastors and Priests have decided to "keep out" of the bedroom, as they say. I'm not suggesting that they come in the bedroom, I'm suggesting they force change in the media that is driving the backseat of the Impala, the high school bleachers, the middle school janitors closet, and the church basement.

In the news as I write these pages, the story is unfolding as University of California at San Francisco launched the online educational course, "Abortion: Quality Care and Public Health Implications." A class which I am told included promoting abortion services as a good career possibility, as future doctors and nurses were being urged to consider specializing in it. We are most likely only a few years away from this being an accepted job offering at the Public School Career Fair. *Maybe there will one day be a Take Your Abortionist To School Day. Maybe the school can present a plaque to the Doctor who kept class sizes lowest and state educational cost to a minimum.* I am not ready for this material to reach the standardized public educational pedagogy. What about you?

Know the greater percentage of abortions are not taking place within the life of married couples. I know there are some exceptions (thanks to ultrasound machines discussed later), but let's start at the major point of the explosion. They are happening because a male person stuck his unprotected maleness where it didn't belong, and now he (and she) wants to get off the hook for it. It is also happening because a woman, or a couple chose to cover up a crime of passion with the albeit legal crime of abortion. *There are no swimming pool accidents.*

My point is that we men have to take some responsibility for how we got into this mess, and the fact we seem to be staying in the mess. I know a big ship is slow to turn, but my challenge is to wake up and start turning it.

This book is not meant to hurt those who have been involved in abortions in the past. Like so many others, many of you were led down an unscrupulous path. You are now coming to understand the effects of that decision. I am not standing in judgment. We are simply addressing the issue now with fuller knowledge. Thanks for staying the course with all of us. I certainly bare the guilt of forty years of avoiding the issue myself. This happened on my watch and I sat back and simply told more jokes.

CHAPTER 5

IT DOES AFFECT MEN

"Try not to become a man of success,
but rather try to become a man of value."
-Albert Einstein

I'm sure there are some men who have had multiple affairs that have ended with multiple abortions and they think nothing of it. But for many of you, reading this book has brought you to remember some things. I offer no apologies. This book is entitled *Awaken The Mighty Men* and not entitled *I'm Okay - You're Okay*. Many of you who have read the pre-publish version have confessed to me that you are now looking back at what you had a part in 30 years ago. Well the good news is that there [is] forgiveness. The best news is that for those who have been forgiven, you have the ability to come along side another man and help him NOT make the same mistake. Those who have been forgiven much have much to show their thankfulness for.

I know there are men who are hurting from the knowledge that they ended a life. It might not have been funded by them. They might not have even known about it for many years after the time. Nevertheless, their child to be was terminated, and it still bothers them. It is called guilt, and from time to time it is good for us. It causes us to be better people and do better things. There's nothing wrong with a little guilt if we are guilty. We all despise the serial killer who goes to his punishment without remorse. Let us all hold ourselves to the same standard.

If 30% of women have an abortion at some time in their life, that puts assigns about 30% to the men as well. So if you are bothered by your past, get some counseling, talk to your Pastor or Priest and find your God provided forgiveness. Then in an act of Godly penance and thanksgiving, go out and do something about it.

CHAPTER 6

TRUTH IS BETTER THAN DAYDREAMS

"The truth is incontrovertible. Malice may attack it, ignorance may deride it, but in the end, there it is."
-Winston Churchill

I know that many men would give me great arguments for the necessity of abortion. I am fully aware of those. I know that some would prefer to sweep this issue under the carpet and let it stay a horrible but acceptable way to eliminate problems. Some might say that I should not give a voice to these arguments. I have nothing to hide. I also don't want anyone to be blindsided by an argument they have not heard. Please note that I can state my personal pro-life stance in these simple words: All life belongs to God - womb to tomb - don't mess with God's stuff. This chapter may be the most fully honest and real discussion of the pro-choice arguments you will ever read in a pro-life publication.

A few years ago I conducted a small survey while preparing for a seminar. I interviewed Pastors as to their [off the record] feelings on abortion. It was very interesting. These conservative Protestants were very strongly opposed to abortion, yet many found themselves unwilling to address the issue within their congregation publicly. Some understood that to bring it up meant that they would or could upset fine church donors. *Having personally spent a few years as a Pastor I know that it is always best to preach against those who are not at the church! Sermon relevance should be limited to blessings only!* Often the Pastor's kindness came from a kind desire. A kindness that did not want to bring up deep wounds that were possessed by women who had had an abortion. For a few the fear stemmed from their own past involvement with it. Fears that in the discussion of this topic their own wife might confess publicly to a past failure.

It is estimated that within the adult female church population, as many as half of those who have had abortions (30% on average) have never told anyone about their abortion. This means that fifteen out of every one hundred [church going] women have never told their Pastor, and certainly not told their children. They still harbor much guilt and shame. It goes un-dealt with, and un-healed, often for an entire lifetime. How many clergy have had an abortion so as not to ruin their chance of landing a job in their desired career during their college and seminary days? Many Pastors know that if this were to be revealed they would lose their job. Let's not be ignorant to the arguments.

I also know that some have a theological bent that says, "We believe that babies go to heaven and unredeemed adults go to Hell." Believing that 90% of adults reject a true faith, they feel it best to just let the children go to heaven. Does this sound crazy to you? There are those, even within the leadership of the Church who hold to this pragmatic approach to theology and abortion. Following this to the fullest mandates we kill all the children to assure them eternal life. Again, I share this so we will not be ignorant to the arguments, even the wildest ones.

I know there are also those who would look at the messed up lives of these abortion minded mothers and ask hard questions. These people question as to why we would want a child to be raised by a mother who has even considered killing that child. Would it be safe to leave a child in that home? What kind of issues would these children face? Let's not be ignorant to the arguments.

I know there are those in conservative parties who are afraid of the [balance of power] implications of overturning Roe vs. Wade. In talking to a number of active republicans, I found deep beneath the "pro-life" talk, a fear of overturning this 1973 legalization. I've heard, "If it were not for Roe vs. Wade we would have 42 million more voting Democrats to contend with and our GOP would be demolished." I can do math. I know that the party most likely has a lot to lose if this happens. This is why many believe we will never truly do anything more than limit late-late term abortions. Some say that deep within the party are the controlling influences that will never allow that to happen.

Understandably, one would think by now, one pro-life President would have at least tried to use his executive order to stop the murder. Right? If only for a season. Why have they not? Why during a recent pro-life presidential term, when both houses were controlled by a pro-life party, was nothing done about this issue. I am told to talk very little about this. I am told it can be dangerous. Cheer up. We will discuss some very well working compromises later in this book. But I share the truth fully so that you may be fully aware. Don't worry, I believe there are answers that can save the child and save conservative values. *I would not have you be ignorant my brothers.* I just want you who are [more] politically aware to not be ignorant to the [all] the arguments, even the real ones.

I could go on to list other [seemingly] acceptable reasons why some argue for abortion. In the end you have to get down to one horrible conclusion. Abortion takes the life of a human being without the consent of that human being. Legalized abortion has established the greatest and most acceptable form of age discrimination. Abortion legalizes the extermination of millions often for the mere reason of inconvenience. It dares to say, "These little people, who we posses full responsibility for their existence, need extermination because we ignorantly did not consider the ramifications of our actions." Dare we kill our children because of our ignorance? I pray we would not continue to use our own ignorance to justify such an atrocity.

What does abortion reveal about the supposed "good and intelligent people" who would kill children for the sake of imposition? What does it say about a nation who would send our young men into battle to save children around the world and not protect the children in their own country? What does it say about the so-called men who stand by and watch this slaughter in Technicolor to the count of over one million bodies in our landfills a year. What does it say about a nation that allows child killing to become a multi-million dollar [for profit] industry under the guise of personal choice? Line them up. Justify it if you can. There is no justification. I tried for years to find a justification. I have tried to work out all the legitimate reasons, and ultimately I could not. I tried to find a loophole. I have read all the scientific information. Even science agrees that abortion stops a beating heart, a heart that beats independently from the mother and at a different rate. Many simply choose to say it is an unfortunate necessary evil. Really? We have gone to war over 3,000 deaths in New York towers when the abortion providers are terminating that many every day. Are we hypocrites? Let's not be ignorant to the plain truth either.

As I stated previously, and for shock value, I like to refer to myself as kinda pro-choice! I simply believe that you need to limit the "choice" to the child... and that is going to take a few years! Men... real men... is it not time we stood up for what is true and right? Turning a deaf ear to the cries of the dying is cowardly. It is more than cowardly, it is a tragedy. Some theologians declare it will become the premier reason for dark remuneration to come upon our nation. When we are at a point of an international abortion of life at the hands of an ISIS will the Creator allow us to receive back what we have been turning a blind eye to? Will this great Creator in that day allow us to receive the reaping of what we have sown? I am not a fear monger... I am not an anarchist... I am a realist... and I'm just asking some questions. What do you think? Look, this subject is tough... wear a cup.

These arguments were included so that you would know the points of your adversary. *Personally, I always hate to be blindsided and I'll bet you do as well.* Do these arguments leave us in a catch 22 situation? No. There are wonderful ways we can go about saving lives within this culture, while we work to bring back moral absolutes to the next generations. There is hope and we will find a way.

No matter which argument you or I might even find the slightest sympathy for, we still come back to the question of whom should determine the length of a human life. I have to always default to my statement: All life belongs to God - womb to tomb - don't mess with God's stuff. I don't want to be any part of being against His authority.

Note: Having previously shared this material in a variety of seminars I understand how this discussion makes many uncomfortable. I am sorry. However, I do believe that for change to come we must be knowledgeable of all the arguments and willing to address each of them no matter how different they are from our belief system. Refusing to acknowledge common beliefs has never made them go away in the past... why should it today?

CHAPTER 7

BACK TO THE FUTURE

"The price of success is hard work, dedication to the job at hand, and the determination that whether we win or lose, we have applied the best of ourselves to the task at hand."
-Vince Lombardi

Many of us have become accustomed to the new sexual standard. Many of us rather enjoy the sexual stimulation of the movies that flood our televisions. Though many of us are even addicts to sexual material on our computers, we need to wake up and do something to stop it. I think that it is time for men to stand up and say, "THIS IS NOT ACCEPTABLE!"

Do you ever watch the History Channel? I was watching a wonderful documentary on the Opium Wars in China. *I'm sure we learned about it in high school, but I was distracted by a really cute girl that semester.* China was on the verge of demise from the widespread opium addiction that had swept the country. The Emperor (whose name I forget), himself now an opium addict, had to step up and call for the elimination of the drug. Though he himself was held in its grip, for the sake of the country, he had to make a decision that was best for his country. He woke up! We must decide to do what is right at all cost.

Some have suggested there are not any males that are really man enough to do that anymore. I believe they are wrong. I hope to heaven that they are wrong. This country is a wonderful, yet wounded ship that is taking on water and we need men to rise up and man the pumps! Man the battle stations! Man the engines. Wake up!

I often recall the inspiring lines from a classic patriotic song. Lines that still shake me to the core. *"Men who will face eternity who aren't afraid to die, Men who will fight for freedom and honor once again..."* We still just need a few good men. This book is my attempt to challenge you to be one of those [few] awake, alive, strong, mighty, good, and great men. It is my challenge to you to stand one day in eternity having "saved lives" as a monument and purpose of your existence. I don't see myself standing before the throne and hearing the great Creator say to me, "You played golf really well, good job!" I want to shape the world. We must wake up and call for a new standard to replace the [no absolute] ideology of the postmodern day!

Chapter 8

A LITTLE LESS SLEEP

"How then shall we live?"
-Francis Schaffer

I am not a picketer! Never have been. I did stand out with my church a couple of times, years ago, on Sanctity of Life Sunday and hold a sign. However good that is, I have come to believe this [battle] will not be won with picket signs, banners, billboards, signs, or bumper stickers.

A reporter from a rather liberal New England newspaper was to call me in a few minutes. As I waited for his call to my hotel room that cold September morning, I watched the news. They were talking about the chemical weapons being used in Syria. The death toll appeared to be over 1300 with many of them being children. They continued the never ending discussion about the fighting in the Middle East, and mainly Iraq. They were asking if we might need to bring back the draft to have enough men to really fight the threat of the week.

Draft? Do you remember that? As a guy who came to adulthood during the Jimmy Carter administration, I remember we all worried about the draft. We were never called. It is almost embarrassing to recount my family military history. My grandfather had WW1, my father had WW2, my uncles had Vietnam, and my cousins had Korea. *My generation had Grenada. Grenada! Do you even remember that battle? It took almost half a day. We jokingly say that we lost a lot of sheep that afternoon.* So my generation (I was born in 1962) does not know [first hand] what it is to lay down our life for a cause, a country, or another person. Some of our younger more recent Gulf War Veterans might have a greater understanding than some of my group. So this was the backdrop for the interview I was about to give.

The phone rang... the soft spoken... slightly lisping voice of the liberal reporter came on the line. I'm guessing that he was at least 15 years younger than me. He greeted me with the normal frivolities that we all say. As a professional (at least I like to think of myself as that) I like to control interviews early if possible. I jumped right into banter, "I'm furious today! Mad! Angry!"

"Why is that Mr. Williams?"

"I'm sitting here watching the news and they are talking about sending our boys and girls into Syria to stop the [so-called] gassing of their own people. Why do we have to send our men and women to die for these people? What have they ever done for us? How would they help us If we needed them?"

"Well Mr. Williams, I'm surprised to hear you say that. Personally, I think that when you consider that many of the people who were gassed, according to the most recent information, were children. We must do something. Certainly we all want to save children?"

"Why do we always have to be the ones to go fight? Let them fight their own battles."

"Maybe we are the only ones right now who have the military capability to do that. Am I correct in believing you are a conservative Mr. Williams? You guys are always wanting to go fight somewhere."

"Well, please call me Mike... I just don't think that we should ask men and women who had nothing to do with this [gassing incident] to give their life for children they don't know. It isn't like I'm ever going to meet one of these kids."

"I like to think as a reporter I am rather neutral, but personally I think that sometimes good and moral people have to do what is not convenient so as to save the masses of humanity. It just seems to be the right thing to do... especially when children are involved."

I responded, "Yes it does... Great... so print that! The great abortion argument is over as well! According to [your own] most excellent logic, it is not too much to ask a woman to give nine months of her life to save the life of a child. Nine months are not too much to endure given the life saving outcome! It is not more than we could expect. You are right, it is the good and moral thing to do. The beauty of this scenario is that we are asking women to give birth to

31

the child that they definitely had a 50% hand in creating. We are not even asking them to sacrifice their life for a stranger. As far as humanity, this act will save the lives of over a million children in the US alone every year. Print that! That is my reason for being in Worcester tonight speaking for the CareNet Clearway Clinic and next week at Assumption College across town."

His demeanor changed. The interview changed. I hope for the first time in his life he saw the simple truth as it came out of his own mouth when he said, "We must do something... certainly we all want to save children."

There may come a time when the United States will have to implement the draft again. There will be those who will run to Canada or Mexico. There will be dissenters. There will also be those, who for the future of life and liberty, will risk their own life for a great length of time to protect the life and liberty of those who cannot protect themselves. They will even risk their lives to protect those who through an abortion would not give themselves to protect the life in their own womb. It is ironic don't you think? I hope by this time you are all saying, "So what shall we do?"

CHAPTER 9

STOP YAWNING, START MOVING

"Our greatest weakness lies in giving up.
The most certain way to succeed is always
To try just one more time."
-Thomas A. Edison

So where do we go from here? That is the proper response question for those of us who are thinkers. *I'm glad Thomas Edison did not reach total befuddlement around his 999th attempt at the light bulb and decide to invent Beer Pong or cheese fondu instead.* Seriously men, what is the best way for us to go forth on this issue and take action? Let's look at what we can do, what we must do, and what we should not do.

Some believe it necessary to restore Intelligent Design to our schools before we can move the sanctity of life to a moral and then legal perspective. Interesting point? Is the answer in simply overturning Roe vs. Wade? I would love to see it! I could pray for that. We certainly need to be a country that is pro-life above pro-convenience. However many don't necessarily believe that laws will solve the problem. Laws rarely work. Think about your own speeding or texting and driving habits. Hmmm, and you are good God-loving, church-attending, flag-waving, constitution-quoting, conservative-voting Americans. I live much of the year in the Dominican Republic where abortion is illegal. We have more abortions per capita than you have. So I understand the point that changing the abortion laws may do little to change this. What can we learn from prohibition of the 1920's? So should we consider that maybe the fight needs to go back further?

These good people ask us to consider that our pro-life / sanctity of life / anti-abortion posture is based on a [morality] of all life being precious and worthy of protection (under God). One Pastor friend of mine believes that when we took God out of our education system, a system that we tell our children to attend and faithfully learn from, we eliminated any sanctity of life. He believes that if we are just educated monkeys, then life has less of a value, and the termination of a life is non-impactful. This is not saying we need to bring back school prayer. We need to bring back to our schools the concept of an Intelligent Designer. If there is an Intelligent Designer, then one day we might stand before that Intelligent Designer to give an account for what we have done with life on the planet. Again, some believe the battle we are fighting is the wrong [primary] battle. Certainly you can't legislate a morality upon the same people you have taught there is no moral absolute! What do you think? Let us not be ignorant of these arguments either.

One good Pastor postulated that Romans chapter eight articulates that [laws alone] will never change society. He argued quite adamantly that no true Christian should rely on the legal system to bring about what only a heart change can accomplish. I seem to remember his repeated phrase, "You cannot make a heart valve start working by simply outlawing heart decease." If you follow a theological argument you might find great connection to his point. He was not for abortion, rather he was under the belief that it would take the Spirit of God moving in the hearts of people to make them live both moral, and life affirming lives. I think he made a real good point. If so, do we waste our time and money on legislation efforts? It could be a legitimate question for those coming from a theological stance. Let's not be ignorant of these arguments either.

Some radicals believe that we should all go "Old Testament" and declare a Jihad (holy war) on the abortionists? Some have done this. It does seem oddly right, yet very wrong to abort the abortionists. We do often put to death those who are convicted multiple murderers, but if this is the case then we would also have to kill everyone who has paid for an abortion. That would have just annihilated 30% of our male population. I don't think the old eye for an eye program has worked very well over the centuries. I am certainly not ready to go to an eye for an eye proposition here. I don't think you have to be a "nut-Job" to be very effective in saving lives and I intend to prove that. So the challenge and my invitation still lives...

On a personal note, I *always desire* to work where I can see quantifiable results. I like to go fishing and catch fish. I don't like to sit in a boat all day and hold a pole! I am a results guy! I have to be working in an area that sees results or I will eventually revert to my lethargic self. Results rule in my world. Am I simply a pragmatist? I like to call it result-driven. What about you?

A Men's bathroom in the St. Louis airport has an interesting little housefly [sticker] attached inside the urinals. *I don't often take photos in public bathrooms, but I have pictures to prove this.* When I first approached the urinal I did not know it was a sticker. I thought it was a housefly. I stood before the urinal, unzipped, wondering why the housefly did not fly away. Then as a man aiming a 45 caliber Colt automatic (which I own a commemorative version of), unleashed the best stream a 52 year old man can. I nailed the fly! But the fly wasn't moving. I kept my stream on it full time. Realizing mid-squirt that my adversary was a sticker, I pushed all the harder trying to remove the sticker from the porcelain receptacle. *The housefly sticker won and I might need to see a Urologist.* This fly sticker intrigued me. I found a maintenance guy for an explanation. "Well Sir, so many men lose focus and pee all over the floor. When we put the housefly stickers on all the urinals exactly where we want the men to aim their pee, this gave men a place to focus. It keeps the floors around the urinals about 500% cleaner." *I'm sure 500% was a slight exaggeration.*

Wow... men need focus... I believe this problem, this situation, this struggle, call it what you will, would be over if we could get enough real men to focus on the issue.

Please keep in mind, this [is] our battle as well. We let this happen. *We sat back and watched Leave It To Beaver, Gunsmoke, The Monkees, Gilligan's Island, The Cosby*

Show, or The Brady Bunch while our Rome burned. We failed. So let's go back and start the fight on the proper front. *Hogan's Heroes should have inspired us to that.*

How can you save the life of a child today? This book has been a waste of time if it does not motivate all of us to accept the challenge and wake up. Let's put a fly sticker on a few areas and see what we can do about the issues.

CHAPTER 10

FAITH WITHOUT WORKS IS DEAD

"It is no use saying, 'We are doing our best.' You have got to succeed in doing what is necessary."
-Winston Churchill

I want to motivate men to involvement, not awareness. Awareness does little, or nothing, or may be even less. Awareness without action creates apathy. I desire men to finish this book awakened with passion over the atrocity of abortion, and the knowledge of how to personally save at least one life a year. I am challenging men to know that they have genuinely done something to stagger abortion statistics in their community of influence by preventing the unnecessary loss of children. I'm not asking men to go to jail or to cover your classic Chevy with pro-life bumper stickers. *That too would be a crime.* I'm asking men to do what is very possible, and in these closing words I want to give men some clear cut strategies for success. Will you be one of those life-saving men?

I am not in any way implying that women are inferior, or incapable. Women have been leading this effort for years and we owe great medals of valor to them for their service. However this book is written to men. I am married to a very intelligent wife who brings great brilliance and strength to my work. This very book would not be in existence without her. Conversely I like to at least think that I bring great strength and intelligence to her work. From the Creator's design we have been made to complete each other. Together we can find complete and intelligent ways to combat this giant. The age-old wisdom reminds us that the sum is greater than the individual parts. Together we are more than we are alone.

There are seven fronts which men can begin to bring about genuine change and life affirming transformation. I will call them *Seven Wake Up Calls*...

1. PREGNANCY RESOURCE CENTER ADVANCEMENT

PRC's need men to become involved and broaden their impact. Men are needed to help usher our centers into the post modern world. Men who will bring business and marketing skills to the Pregnancy Resource Centers and aid them in operating on a contemporary plane. Many of these good organizations are 10 - 20 years behind the curve (as often seen in religious based organizations). Some are as postmodern and efficient as the milk churn. Men are needed to locate, enhance, and secure financial security.

2. COMPREHENSIVE SEXUAL INTEGRITY EDUCATION

Men are needed to help re-think and rewrite the sexual integrity curriculum being given to students. We need to honestly address all aspects, and truly address even that which makes us uncomfortable. Men are needed to help address uncomfortable issues.

3. INTELLIGENT VISION TO POLITICAL ACTION ORGANIZATIONS

Men are desperately needed to bring new and strategic vision to organizations who have been accused of being little more than political fundraising entities. Men are needed to instill tactical events that will genuinely bring about life saving legislation.

4. MEN'S MENTORING PROGRAMS

Men are needed to personally mentor the male counterpart of the women who are in the educational process with the local Pregnancy Resource Center. When we reach the men who are the fathers of the children, we secure a good future for the children the PRC has saved.

5. ADOPTION ADVOCACY AND ASSISTANCE

We need men who will bring business skills to the adoption organizations. Men who will find ways to overcome roadblocks and streamline the adoption process.

6. Creation of More Pregnancy Homes

We need men to build and help operate homes for girls threatened with homelessness due to pregnancy. Some parents use the threat of homelessness to force their children to have an abortion. Some (often church member) parents are more concerned with their reputation than they are the life of an unborn child. Pride is an angry killer. Where are my men who can operate a hammer and saw? We need some men on the roof.

7. Exposing the Need in and Through Local Churches

We need men who will stand up in their local congregation to assure the needs of post abortive women and men are addressed through post abortion recovery programs. Men need to encourage the Pastors and Priests to address sanctity of life issues with honesty and grace.

I trust these honest observations and postulations will provide practical ways men can help bring about the needed boost to achieve success in saving the lives of children. These seven areas need awake men! Let's define in greater detail the seven areas in which I feel we need to awaken our new offensive line. This might get a little controversial.

LET'S PUT HANDLES ON IT

"It's not what you look at that matters, it's what you see."
- Henry David Thoreau

I. PREGNANCY RESOURCE CENTER ADVANCEMENT

Every man can get involved with a local CareNet or Heartbeat affiliated Pregnancy Resource Center (often referred to as a PRC). These organizations are not picketers, they simply open their doors to pregnant daughters and granddaughters who are exploring the possibilities of an abortion. They help girls understand the long term ramifications of abortion and the many life affirming alternatives. They do promote with passion the giving of nine months of their life for the greater good of a child all the while not condemning those who chose poorly. They stand as a place of healing for those who have experienced an abortion, and are now facing the emotional effects of that abortion. Additionally they are often the local provider of Abstinence / Sexual Integrity based education to public and private schools. These PRC's also mentor / educate men on how to become a great father for their children. The continuing education provided by the PRC's literally transform "at-risk" families to thriving! Many of these organizations provide STD/STI testing. This brings sons and daughters into personal counseling through their own concern from their own sexual practices. This testing service allows them to assume a mentorship role with these young people who come in to be tested. This allows these young persons to make better future choices. These PRC organizations are operated by good people with a good mission and are having an extremely quantifiable effect. Many refer to the PRC movement as the only greatly successful arm of the pro-life world.

These PRC's also reach out to the granddaughter who woke up one morning after a college party pregnant. Before we get too judgmental let us remember that it required the involvement of somebody's grandson for this to happen. It was not an unforeseeable accident by any stretch of the imagination. Many of our daughters given this situation will fall into the category of Abortion Minded or Abortion Vulnerable. Many emotions will make them vulnerable to abortion, one is a fear of what you, yes you, and the rest of the family will think.

So you will know, *Abortion Minded* and *Abortion Vulnerable* are terms that are used in the pro-life world and as a man you need to understand them. An *abortion minded* daughter is one who, after finding out she is pregnant goes out in search of an abortion. Many times this is sought with no information given to the father of the child. Many times it is with the expressed permission and financing of the father. Often these daughters find themselves in the local PRC for the Free Pregnancy verification services provided. While at the PRC the staff will be able to share with them the whole truth about the life that is inside of them. After seeing an ultrasound of their [so called] blob of tissue 80% of them realize that this is a viable life inside of them and choose to do the best thing for the child. Often women come to the local center thinking it is an abortion provider... good... it pulls them through the front door. *I am a fisherman... I understand why we use bait and not just a silver barbed hook. If I can justifiably use artificial lures to get a catfish for nothing more than the fun of catching it, I should certainly use these techniques to save lives.*

The *abortion vulnerable* daughter is one with great desire to do the right thing. However, in the course of her 40 weeks of pregnancy, something could easily happen that will cause her to question whether or not she could handle having a baby. There are a number of reasons some of our daughters chose to abort after first desiring to keep the child. It can be finances, a boyfriend's threats of abandonment, continued pressure from either family, or even fear of losing the dream career. These are all based in fear. Even more dangerous, the abortion vulnerable daughter is also one who does not have good mentoring and support all through the 40 weeks of pregnancy. The abortion vulnerable daughter is said to be the most likely to have the extremely tragic and dangerous late term abortions. These obtain a late term abortion though they had originally intended to birth the child. The fear filled and unsupported young lady can vacillate from giving life to choosing death in a short time without an intervention.

Some believe abortions are not taking place in [small town] America. They would be surprised to know the facts. In fact, the rural communities are where the scourge of abortion is often deeply hidden. Old fashioned pride is touching the heartland with deadly consequences to the children of the heartland.

Within the PRC we desperately need men, businessmen who understand marketing to help the PRC's develop a strategy of reaching these clients. Men need to bring contemporary business tactics to a work that is heavily dominated by very nice women who are kind and always encouraging. We need men who will offer another perspective on touching the life of the client. Men understand hunting and fishing, and hunting and fishing is the skill needed to reach abortion minded / abortion vulnerable clients. This is the first task of the PRC! You are needed on your local PRC board or volunteer group. Is this your place of service?

I write these last six paragraphs with great respect for the female majority who have held this Pregnancy Resource Center battle line for many years. They have fought long and hard and saved literally thousands of lives. I am honored to call so many of these ladies (and a few men) my respected friends. These wake up calls to men are meant to bring new and fresh arms to reinforce the fight they have been in for longer than I. These wake up calls are meant to bring supplies to the weary. These wake up calls are to bring men into the well oiled machine of the PRC's and help them achieve victory in the goal they started with.

2. COMPREHENSIVE SEXUAL INTEGRITY EDUCATION

Many PRC's and some private organizations go into public and private schools to teach (and legitimatize) a rather unpopular concept. They create educational programs that share an alternative approach to rampant uncontrollable human sexuality... and they call it Abstinence Education. It is a simple tried and true method of waiting until you are married before you participate in baby making acts. I am told that many men, even within the Christian faith, do not believe in abstinence. I have to admit that with the media, music, and movies pumping the sexual revolution as if it were the norm, we do face a large foe. But nevertheless David faced Goliath and won. We know that for many students they [will be able] to withstand the pressures and truly find joy in abstinence. There are quantifiable stats on that. We must teach our sons and daughters that they are not just animals in heat.

I recently had a man approach me at an event and tell me that he did not believe that abstinence education worked, even though he was supporting the Pregnancy Center who was providing the program. I questioned his motives. He explained that he did believe that it slowed down the age at which young women were becoming sexually involved. He believed that moving sexual encounters from middle school to at least a high school or college age level would lower the pregnancy rate. His rational was that high schoolers and college aged students were more apt to use condoms. You may not agree with his premise, but I am thankful for his financial support of the process. No matter your viewpoint, I'll bet that you would love to find an abstinent boy for your own daughter. Everyone knows that condoms can break. Every man and woman knows there are no condoms for the emotions of the soul. Every man secretly desires their wife to have kept herself pure for them.

Sexual education has to be offered to our sons and daughters that challenge them to sexual purity. Will all students be able to achieve it? Certainly not all, we can't even keep it pure among the clergy these days. Nevertheless, just because it will not take hold for some, does not mean we should deny it to others. I have talked to many many students who have told me of their commitment to abstinence and how it was made at one of these PRC provided Abstinence Education classes. I have met those in college who tell me that they are now getting ready to graduate as the "non-sex freak", although a happy non-pregnant, non-STD/STI, non-sex Freak!

Maybe I am walking where angels fear to tread, but I want to go further. My inbox may be filled with your letters right now. Some are quietly saying we need a more balanced-sense approach to our education. Admittedly I do tend to go for hard-right or extreme-left when sometimes the answer is on another plane. Here is a letter I received a few months ago.

Dear Mr. Williams,

I saw your abstinence program at a public school program in Kentucky last week. May I create for you a scenario? Your daughter is on date number 100 with a guy she has been now dating for three years. You have allowed it because you like the guy. He's college material. He might make a good partner in your business someday. This wonderful guy, who like all those around him has been so extremely sexually pumped up throughout his school years that each day he lives on the brink of explosion. The same supercharging could be said for your innocent little daughter, though you may not want to admit it. Do you want them, if they fall victim to lust, heat, passion, or stupidity... do you want them to fail wearing a condom, or to make this grave mistake without a condom? Wait... forget the supposed religiously correct response... nobody is reading this but you and me... do you want to at least protect your daughter from an STI or pregnancy? Think about the kids who are getting no good influence at home. How are they going to deal with the pressure? If King David, the man after God's own heart couldn't keep his manliness in his robe... how will sexually supercharged sixteen-year-old regular David do it? King David was listed in God's Hall of Faith after his moral failure. We need straight talk in this area. You are a Christian speaker who should be bringing help to everyone not just the good little homeschool Christian kids from great homes who will find out about sex on their wedding night. I look forward to your response.

Thank You,
(obviously I am removing the name)

Ouch! How would you have answered his question? I might answer that it is hard to bring the full truth to a public school that won't let you talk about intelligent design, or absolutes in morality. *As a man, I most always have some sort of comeback, even if it is nothing more than deferring.* I responded to his letter with a simple... good point!

I once met an abstinence educator who turned down becoming the so-called sex-ed guru in her public school district because she would be required to also tell them how to put a condom on a banana. In addition to teaching condom installation technique she could also teach abstinence as the best option, and talk about the failure rate of condoms. Was she wise in leaving the kids with no good abstinence information so that she could stand on her [so-called] holy ground? I agree that we need some of you to help develop the next generation of real life abstinence education that works for men and women. Yes, I know this is tough talk... but you are a man... you are supposed to take the challenges. I know the damage that sex outside of marriage does to both people. I know the future [un-bondable] consequences and all that can entail. I have written an entire book about the pro's of abstinence! However, if abstinence is failed in achieving, do we need to add pregnancy or an STD to their problems? I don't have all the answers, but I agree we need some men to step up and start addressing it. We will in ten more years, when we see where we have failed thus far. Why not save ten years of students and deal with it now? This is coming from a guy who will speak to over 5000 students next week and proclaim abstinence is the best possible way to go. I believe in abstinence! That is what I teach. I'm just saying that maybe we need some men to honestly step up and bring reality to our highest hopes.

3. Intelligent Vision to Political Action Organizations

Men are needed who actively assist various Right to Life organizations and our other pro-life politically driven organizations. These organizations need help directing their path for actions that bring success. We need men who will do more than simply raise money, to raise more money, to raise money for awareness, to raise more money. We are all deeply aware! We need men to bring accountability for results. I have many friends who are deeply involved in this work and I love them dearly. We must call for greater assessment of all of our works. Inspection is what makes us better. If I kept taking money from you to fix your car, you would expect me to one day fix it. You would not pay me to simply bring awareness of your engine problems.

We need to have men who will stand up to the politicians who have been receiving the pro-life voter support (and money in many cases) and call them on the carpet. We need men who stand at the door of pro-life candidates and get them moving. I rode to a pro-life event the other day with bright young man and his wife. My driver brought up an interesting point in asking me what the last [so-called] pro-life U.S. Presidents have done for the movement? Have we had one executive order from any of them? He made a good point. We need men who will take our pro-life message off the bumper stickers and put it into a working world situation. We need genuine brains behind the sound bites and behind Pro-Life Rally! If insanity is doing the same thing and expecting different results, could we call our political / legislative direction insane?

A pastor friend of life believes that instead of spending millions each year to [supposedly] overturn Roe vs. Wade, we should work on making the adoption process so simple that all those desiring a child can have that happen. Instead of funding abortions, the state could fund adoptions for the hundreds of thousands of people who would love to parent a child. He believes this could be the most effective attainable agenda. Is he totally wrong?

A multimillionaire friend of mine believes that the issue will only change when we properly educate the public about abortion. He says, "Our current ABORTION IS MURDER signage does not change someone's heart. Our losses prove that. So how can we in good conscience continue on the same path?" He advises that we invest our millions of pro-life political dollars is creating television media to move the public opinion. I explained to him that the Vitae Caring Foundation produces excellent videos for this but lacks the funding to distribute them to major markets.

One PRC director told me that both arms of this sanctity of life movement needs to work together to bring about legislation to protect the work of the PRC's. This truly would allow both parties to be involved in genuinely saving lives in a boots on the ground fashion. I found that to be an interesting assessment. *Unity among those [religious persons] who were supposed to be known by their unity has always been a major problem since 1054 (you theologians understand the date). I have days when I wonder if we really prefer the joys of fighting to the joys of a unity.*

Earlier in this book I mentioned the pastor who believes our pro-life investment needs to be in bringing back "Intelligent Design" as an alternative theory of existence. This would or could help returning the sanctity of life to an acceptable moral platform. Does the political / legislative arm of our sanctity of life organizations need to re-focus? We need to take a serious look at the battles we are fighting and ask the right questions. This may not get us on Fox News or CNN but it might just be where we need to start to solve the problem. But maybe it would get us on there more!

Another pastor friend believes that the legislative arms of the pro-life movement need to refocus on parental consent requirements. Instead of spending millions each year to [supposedly] overturn Roe vs. Wade, he believes we focus on legislation that requires parental notification of a child under 18 seeking the very [medical] procedure of abortion. In a world where we can't give an aspirin to a child without parental signatures and notarized statements, it just seems ludicrous that this same daughter that you could not give an aspirin, can have her fetus injected with salt water through her own stomach, the baby sucked out of her uterus, limb from limb with a vacuum, and this done without parental notification. What level of legislative stupidity is this? In some states this has been achieved. Awesome! Excellent job! This truly was strategic, intelligent, and successful legislation.

Sometimes good zealots take on the largest mountain (Roe vs. Wade) instead of simply tunneling through it. We need men who will bring wisdom to the table and not accept the status quo. We need men who will cause funding to go to where it works and not simply where it brings headlines for future fundraisers. We need men who will ask the tough questions about all of our organizations and demand that we work at a high level and produce results. *George Washington, Thomas Edison, and Steve Jobs would be unknown names in history if it was not for their success.* It seems that in every business except for church / para-church / para-political, if the leadership is not getting the goal accomplished, they would be replaced. Let's find leadership that can win... or hire a ringer!

FYI: I write these words on Nov 5, 2014. We have just experienced a change in the ruling political power party. The Democrats, who are blamed for pro-choice agenda no longer control the vote. Let's see what happens. Let's see if the Republican Party will actually bring any substantial legislation to the table. Let's see if our pro-life organizations will demand action or sit idly by as they did last time this power reversal was experienced. Pay attention and watch, man. I might have to eat these words in a few weeks. I hope so. I pray so. I hope this new order will prove me to be an idiot. But I am betting that without men standing up and forcing the GOP to make good on their pro-life promises, my statements will stand for a long time.

Speaking recently with a PRC leader in Michigan I was presented with an interesting hypothesis. She explained that if it were not for the legalization of abortion, all the abortions would be done in secret, and women would not be openly walking into a clinic like theirs for help. In other words, according to her, if we force abortions underground, there would be no way (theoretically) to reach the women with an abortion alternative option. You can call her crazy, but her reasoning works on paper. I remind you that I live most of my year in the Dominican Republic where abortion is illegal. When I say that, pro-lifers on all sides of the isle cheer. Wait a minute, I am told that we have more abortions per capita than in countries where it is legal. Many abortions are stopped each year as women unknowingly go into a PRC thinking that group offers abortion. While on the ultrasound table they are counseled about the truth of life and shown the beating heart of the supposed blob of tissue. Their mind is changed approximately 80% of the time. If abortion is not above ground, we may lose a lot of women and children. This is a very interesting hypothesis if nothing else.

Newton's third law of motion reminds us that for every action - there is an equal and opposite reaction. We must look at the outcomes of what we are trying to do before we try to do it. I was given a great illustration of this last October while standing in front of an Ultrasound vendor company booth at a national conference. These amazing ultrasound units that are being sold to us by these [so-called] wonderful pro-life companies, by wonderful [so-called] pro-life salesmen, are the same units they sell to doctors who use them to promote abortion. These doctors use the machines to speculate that a child might have a birth defect. So what? That is a major contributing factor to our American abortion rate. The machine that we use to save lives is possibly causing more abortions than it saves. Why do I mention that? We need to remember that not every [so-called] great idea is the best idea. There is much to consider to bring intelligence and not just knee-jerk reactions to all of our life affirming operations. We must create a place of effective strategy for our battle. For every action...

I was part of an interview with former Planned Parenthood director Abby Johnson last week. She now speaks nationally and chairs a pro-life organization in Austin, Texas. She said there were almost sixty (60) other groups in the Austin area raising funds for their slight variation on the pro-life theme. Sixty? Yes, she said sixty. I went back and checked the recording. And that was in the Austin area alone. Do those stats play out nationally? I am afraid to ask. With this understanding, maybe another starting point would be to work as a unified team.

4. MEN'S MENTORING PROGRAMS

Every PRC needs men who will mentor men. Many of the boyfriends need someone to teach them how to become a real man and a real father. Many are in this position because they never personally had any good parenting. Men by nature, are born to be mentors. We need to be in positions of teaching. It makes us feel good! It fulfills our God given instincts of leadership. Your local PRC needs men who will offer their mentoring skills to the father clients. These young immature men need a man to talk to about life and fathering. They need a male voice to encourage them to wake up as a father and take on their responsibility as a father. We can complain about the way society is going, but until we step up and help fallen society change we are just as guilty, but on another level. It is one thing for the stupid to be stupid, however we who have been blessed with wisdom should hold ourselves to a higher standard of service.

I spoke last week to Kirk Walden author of the phenomenal book entitled *The Wall: Rebuilding a Culture of Life in America and Ending Abortion as We Know it.* I asked him how he would encourage men to escalate the fight for the true sanctity of life. He responded, "By creating mentoring initiatives for new fathers--many who likely have never had a relationship with their own fathers. More than 80% of women who are victims of abortion say that if the father had been supportive of their pregnancies, they would have likely chosen life. By reaching these young dads, men can be the leaders in turning our culture around, toward life." Wow, that was some interesting insight. We can directly impact the next generational round of abortion in America by creating a culture of good fathers. The local PRC brings to us young fathers who are crying out to be mentored. Will you look these young men in the face and answer their call?

For the last umpteen years we have watched as [maleness] has been disintegrating to the evolution of some variation of either a biped sloth or a limp wristed metrosexual. It is time we men acted on the need to change direction. Pardon the spirituality here, but I believe it was Jesus who put it quite directly saying, "To the person who has been given much - much is required." Is mentoring men a place where you could give 4 hours a month? What other area of challenge are you currently serving in that would prohibit this? How are you currently giving back to the great Creator God?

5. Adoption Advocacy and Assistance

I heard the famed conservative comedian say, "These pro-life people need to adopt a few of these babies and not pompously tell women what to do." *Don't take that as a direct quote. It was from my memory.* The truth is that a lot of good people [are] adopting and if the legal system were more efficient, that would happen a lot more often. We need legislation that makes the adoption process easier and less expensive. We need to forge ahead without getting bogged down in the side issues of what kind of couple should be allowed to adopt. We religious people can so allow the enemy to sidetrack us. I know this is a hot button issue, but so is the need to get children into good homes. I don't want to stand before God having kept [thousands] of children unadopted for fear that [hundreds] would be adopted by [non-religious / non-Christian] couples. Let's be honest, heterosexual Christians have done as much to destroy the [sanctity of marriage] as the liberal left. Let's wake up with honesty. Glitches will always distract those who are ignorant or not truly committed. Do the most good! *Good may be the enemy of great, but good is a lot better than bad. I hope they put that quote on my tombstone. My wife says she might.*

Now along with enacting legislative change to the adoption laws, have you ever thought about adopting a child? OUCH! That came out of the blue didn't it? I know that kind of commitment is not for everyone, but it is for some of you to think about. Could you and your spouse take on a child who needs you? Is adoption your place of prolife / pro-child action? *Here's a bumper sticker idea: Pro-Choice... Choose Adoption!*

6. Create More Pregnancy Care Homes

Live out your genuine pro-life viewpoint by creating more PCH's or serving the needs of an existing Pregnancy Care Home. These are houses that have been set up to take in young girls who are pregnant and have nowhere to turn. Their families might be unable to help them. Often these daughters have been forced to leave their homes by parents who are embarrassed with the situation. How in this modern free love - free sex - friends with benefits society that we elders have ushered in, could we ever stand in judgment of others? Knowing those I grew up with, I know of few moms or dads who can stand up to scrutiny of complete sexual purity. The internet has lost that for most young men by the time they turn twelve. *Don Henley was right in calling this age the "End Of The Innocence."* These Pregnancy Care Houses need husbands and wives who will come and mentor the daughters of this generation and see transformation in their life. They need painters, and mowers, and weekend house sitters. Is this how you could best serve your pro-life profession?

As with any of these great needs among true pro-life men comes the ability to understand our own personal failures. These daughters and sons don't need perfect role models, they need transparent hearts who will help them charter the course of life. They need replacement fathers and replacement mothers who will help them learn to be a good father or a good mother. We don't need those who have never failed. In fact, this calling is filled with those who have failed, and failed at least enough to have compassion on those who have become a victim of looking for love in all the wrong places.

7. Exposing the Need in Local Churches

Male elders and deacons need to give the pastors and priests encouragement (and permission) to talk about the issues. They need to respectfully push their pastors to present the full good news to the full body of Christ. Your pastor needs to know that he and his family are safe and forgiven if they have been involved with this in the past.

Your priest needs you to support him in presenting the pro-life truth. They need to be safe in being honest.

My grandfather had an old rimless tractor tire on his farm. The boy cousins loved to combine our strength to take this six foot tall rubber treaded beast to the top of the hill. As a game, we would roll it down the hill [at] each other. *I'm not saying everything you do as a kid is very smart.* No matter how big I got, I could never put my arm out to stop the rolling tire dead in its tracks. It was rolling too fast and it was too heavy. I did learn that I could run alongside and get if off balance. It would then turn itself off its intended course. Newton's First Law of Motion reminds us that changing the current motion of any organization (and I compare these laws loosely) will require a greater amount of force. Rolling stones are hard to stop, and even harder to move in another direction. Will you be man enough to bring new intelligence and refocus to the sanctity of life movement? I would dare those of you currently in these groups to read this chapter out loud to the men attending your next meeting. We need sanity working hand in hand with sanctity! C.S Lewis aptly said, "You are never too old to set another goal or to dream a new dream."

1 - 7. IMPERATIVE ADDITION TO EACH

To each of the above we need to add intelligent prayer. I do not include prayer as if it is a non-important option, but rather I see it as a fully connected part to each area. Prayer is important! I know that this is not the special gift many men are blessed with. I understand that. I have been told that by many of you. Many men see prayer as a designated time where they sit in a room for multiple hours as [more verbally articulate] women talk to God about what they believe that God is most likely already aware of. *I have often sarcastically commented after a hearing someone inform God that "Sister Sherry was experiencing a headache and needs a special touch," that God might be saying, "Wow, I did not know that. Thanks for telling me... and thanks for giving me an idea about what to do for her... I would not have thought about that!"* If God is all knowing (and I believe He is), then prayer must be more than informing God what is going on like a daily newscast.

Let me bring prayer to light in this way. Dan Rather once asked Mother Teresa of Calcutta about her prayer ritual. She explained that when she prayed she did not say anything, she just listened. For those of you afraid of public prayer, no problem, for public prayer has yet to overturn Roe Vs. Wade and it has been publicly named and claimed by some of the top Christian leaders in the country. Our issue needs men who will pray by silently listening to God and waiting for His inspired wisdom. I hope the list above will give you a place to start. As Jeremiah Johnson said, *"Anyone can get knocked down to the floor at an altar in a religious ceremony, but where are those who will take a stand for what is true and right on the altar of daily life?"*

Again we are not asking men to take up the banner because it has been dropped by women. On the contrary... women have been holding up the banner! It is time that we came together to provide what only we [together] can find... wholeness to our work. When we combine our diverse gifting, we see that the sum is greater than the parts.

All of these issues are intertwined. Each one connects to the other. Some require the other to be involved for both to be successful. I am asking God for creativity. We need to find creative [new] approaches to face the challenges of postmodern society. The centuries have proved men to be the most creative, inventive, ingenious creatures ever endowed by the greatest Creator of all. The centuries have proved us to be much like the One in who's image we have been created... and that is creative. Please take up the fights and the arguments where I have left off. I know that many of you have the ability to take the seeds that I have planted and take it to the next level. Go for it with my blessings. Man... it is your turn at the plate... swing for the fence!

CHAPTER 12

CHANGE FOR CHANGE

"Infuse your life with action. Don't wait for it to happen. Make it happen. Make your own future. Make your own hope. And whatever your beliefs, honor your Creator, not by passively waiting for grace to come down from upon high, but by doing what you can to make grace happen... yourself, right now, right down here on Earth."
- Bradley Whitford

Change For Change is my new basic - bottom line motto. It sounds almost presidential don't you think? Here is the bottom line. If you can do nothing more from the action list above, here is where you [can] start today. You can personally save the life of one child this year for a very small amount. Your local PRC can reach an abortion minded / abortion vulnerable client, help her make a life plan for the child, undergo extensive parenting / transformation classes, and deliver that child to life for a center expense of between seven hundred and eleven hundred dollars per child. Yes, a donation of $2 or $3 a day rescues one child. If you could find $2 or $3 a day (maybe in pocket change) from your lunch, you could truly be an active and genuine pro-life person. Could a REAL MAN like yourself could go back to a fifty cent *cup of Joe?* Could you save two bucks a day by not buying a *"Mocha Grande Half-Caff Soy Goat Milk Hazelnut Light Foam Limp-Wrist Blend, with a caramel swirl"* and save one child this year? *Sorry if that sounded sarcastic!* If we all did that for ten years... wow... hundreds of thousands of children could be transformed from the waste basket to life, and their mothers and fathers could have their lives radically altered for good. I personally find the extra I need by not giving to the requests that come in every day for random (never heard of) fundraisers. I chose to focus on making my spare change count for a sure valuable shot! Focus your effort on where you can truly be successful.

We have got to start somewhere. I have given you seven places to start our transformative process for the sanctity of life. I give you "Change for change" as a minimal involvement while we are working and thinking and serving and saving. Are you in? *Rattle that pocket. Wake up mighty man... and do it with cheaper coffee.*

CHAPTER 13

NOW THAT WE ARE OUT OF BED

"Do you want to know who you are? Don't ask. Act! Action will delineate and define you."
- Thomas Jefferson

Let me thank you for being man enough to read this far. You are better than most. Reward yourself today. Our world is filled with apathy and you have shown yourself to be above that. You have my respect. We really can do something to bring about change. From the days of my youth I remember a powerful song in which the lines declared, *"I want to be a man you would write about... a thousand years from now you would read about."* I have come to hope that those words can be more than just dramatic BS or hyperbole. I'll bet you hope for that also.

In the final years of former President Ronald Reagan's life he lost much of the energy and swagger of his early life. This once charismatic leader was now in his physically, and mentally declining years. This will most likely come for all of us if we get the opportunity to live long enough. In these final years he spent much of his time around his familiar and famed Presidential Library in California. There are many heartwarming stories from those days, but one moves me to this very day.

Many people toured this library that celebrated his rather impressive achievements. They still do. During President Reagan's declining years he would come each day to his office at the library. He would busy himself making notes and scurrying about. To honor him they would usually bring at least one tour group by to visit him, even though his mental health had greatly decayed. Visitors at that time have written and recounted their experience with the aging President time and time again. Many days he could not remember being President of the most powerful nation on the earth. Many days he could not remember his movie career that spanned decades. Many days he could not remember those words that rocked the world proclaiming to the famed General Secretary of the Communist Party, "Mr. Gorbachev, tear down this wall." Those milestones were sadly gone from his memory. They say that he would rise from his desk often oblivious to the guest's questions and take them to a little picture on the wall. A picture that he always remembered. The picture came from his youth in 1926 as a lifeguard at Lowell Park, back in Illinois. He would proclaim proudly his heritage to those gathered in that office, "I saved seventy-seven lives that summer." He [always] remembered that even though his very illustrious Presidential legacy was now alluding him. Wow... here is an icon of a man who could be remembered for so many things and yet the legacy that he takes with himself to the end was the saving of seventy-seven young lives.

Do I need to explain that illustration to you? I hope not. *I can explain it to you, but I can't understand it for you!* This President Reagan illustration challenges me to wake up! It challenges you to wake up! It challenges us to all to wake up and do what we can to save lives because in the end that is really what counts. What will your legacy be? Do you have a seventy-seven life picture yet? You still can.

I want to be remembered as a life saver, because I was a life saver. I want to stand one day before a Creator having many daughters and sons standing with me... the children I helped save. I challenge you to join me. I challenge you to surpass my efforts. I challenge you to make a difference. I challenge you to be the one who turns the tide. I challenge you to be the one who brings smart legislation that causes change and not just hype and awareness. I challenge you to bring new life to the PRC movement by your involvement. I challenge you to call the liberal and conservative politicians on the carpet. I challenge you to find the new ways of communicating sexual integrity to our students. I challenge you to find ethical ways of protecting those who will make mistakes. I challenge you to open the next pregnancy home. I challenge you to cut the red tape and expense of adoption. I challenge you to be the one who saves a child every year with your pocket change. I challenge you to wake up. We broke the back of American slavery at Appomattox. We stopped the Nazi regime at Stalingrad. We recovered from the attack on Pearl Harbor. The list could go on. Let's fix this.

Do I have a personal interest in this other than to move a few books for a few dollars? Good question. I should have answered this sooner. For your information, I receive no royalties on this book! However I do have a vested interest in this subject. You see I consider myself a rescued kid! I am an adopted kid. But that was not my initial reason for involvement in this cause. In 1998 my wife and I chose adoption for our first child. Not because we had to, but because we wanted to say thanks to God in response to my adoption in 1962. I never saw myself as a speaker for this movement until the day in 2001 that I received a call from Dr. Dobson's office and was invited to speak at a Focus On The Family Conference. At that point I had to make a choice. I loved my career and my work, but I was called to wake up, and make a difference. I'm sure glad I did. My further participation was secured when our adopted son, at a Sanctity of Life prayer vigil, pointed to the padlocked medical containers behind the security fence, located behind the abortion center. With tears in his eyes he said, "Daddy, that's what they wanted to do to me..." Now you understand my vested interest...

My wife loves the theater. After many years she finally drug me to see *Les Miserables*. And *miserable* I was, well at least for the first half until I took a nap. *For the record I think the movie was much better.* It is a truly wonderful story of the fight between good and evil. Near the end of the presentation the remaining [good] resistance fighters rally around a common song. I can still hear the choir of fighters, *"Who will join in our crusade? Who will be strong and stand with me? Somewhere beyond the barricades is there a world you long to see?"* The crowd at this point was singing along, waving, standing, shouting as if we were actually cast members ourselves there fighting upon the barricades. *I'm just saying that lighters were in the air.*

Man... you were created for more battles than a fantasy football league, an occasional golf game on weekend, or even a motivational Civil War reenactment. You were created for greatness. Men... awakened men... real men... let's roll... let's go. There is a line in the sand. I challenge you to cross it and throw that sand in the eyes of the enemy. I challenge you to make a difference. I challenge you to become involved in the resistance. I challenge you to help secure a victory. I challenge you to lead the next battle, maybe the final one. Like a contemporary Prophet Joel, I challenge you to beat your business skills, your trade skills, your craftsmanship, your intelligence into swords and start swinging them. Will you be brave and fight with us? Will you join in our crusade? Let's change the current course of human history.